Keeping Love Alive

Keeping Love Alive

Thoughts and Tips for Strengthening Your Marriage

Cyndi Haynes

**Andrews McMeel
Publishing**

Kansas City

This book is dedicated to my editor, Jean Zevnik Lucas,
who just happens to be a recent bride.
May your love always burn brightly.

01 02 03 04 05 BIN 10 9 8 7 6 5 4 3 2 1

Library of Congress Cataloging-in-Publication Data
Haynes, Cyndi.
  Keeping love alive : thoughts and tips for strengthening your marriage
/ Cyndi Haynes.
      p. cm.
  ISBN 0-7407-1966-1 (pbk.)
    1. Marriage—Miscellanea. I. Title.

HQ734 .H197 2001
306.81—dc21

                                                    2001022653

ACKNOWLEDGMENTS

I wish to thank all of the wonderful people at Andrews McMeel Publishing for believing in this book. You all are an author's dream, and I appreciate all of your hard work on my behalf more than I can say.

I also want to thank my agent, Jimmy Vines, for his enthusiasm and dedication to my career. I look forward to a lifelong partnership with you.

Dear Reader,

It is my most sincere wish that you find within these pages insight and inspiration to create the marriage of your dreams.

The current divorce statistics are extremely disheartening. One out of two first marriages end in divorce. More than sixty percent of second marriages and seventy percent of third marriages end in divorce.

If you are reading this book, that tells me that you are interested in keeping your love life alive, and that is half the battle.

I wish for you many, many happy anniversaries!

Cyndi Haynes

An ounce of prevention
is worth a pound of cure.

Ben Franklin

Focus on giving to your partner instead of getting
something from your partner.

෧෨

In spite of difficulties, always be
your authentic self.

෧෨

Stop:
nagging
whining
complaining
View your marriage as a sacred gift from God.

෧෨

Help your spouse to "save face" whenever you can.

෧෨

Be nice to all of your in-laws.

Forget about all of the efforts you made yesterday.
After all, your mate is much more interested in
what you are trying to do today.

Have faith in:
yourself
dreams
goals
abilities

Believe in yourself; every ear vibrates
to that iron string.

Ralph Waldo Emerson

Speak from abundant love rather than
a lack of love.

Become an uplifting force in your mate's successes.

Always take the moral high road.

Beat the odds; don't become part of
the 50 percent of marriages that end in divorce.

Confront problems before fear sets in
and paralysis takes over.

Learn the fine art of disagreeing peacefully.
Learn how to argue and still show respect
and kindness to your mate.

Try to share a common vision of your union.

Walk away from disagreements whenever you are:
tired
stressed
overly emotional

Love is a great teacher.

Saint Augustine

Recommit yourselves to each other
on a monthly basis.

೧౨

Always look for the meeting ground when you and
your mate disagree. Find the happy medium.

೧౨

Remember that your mate is only human.

Make a list of three activities or topics
that you and your mate have been avoiding.
Is there a common theme?

What steps can you take today to have
a positive impact on these areas?

Try to view a disagreement as a time to be
thankful that your mate thought enough of you
to take the time and effort to share her side
of the story with you.

Don't lie—honesty really is the best policy.

Practice what you preach or stop preaching it.

Each relationship you have with
another person reflects the relationship
you have with yourself.

Alice Deville

Keep in mind that the more respect you show
for your spouse, the more respect you will receive
from your spouse.

❦

Develop objectivity. Look at the facts.

❦

Remember when you point the finger of blame
at your spouse, you still have three fingers
pointing back at you.

Stop putting off doing the necessary steps
that you know you need to do to improve things
in your marriage.

Make sure that you and your mate both
have credibility with each other, for it is the
very foundation of a quality marriage.

Anxiety is love's greatest killer.

Anaïs Nin

Surround yourselves with family members and
friends who support your marriage.

Listen to your mate with your full attention.

Become passionate about your own life
and this will draw your mate even closer to you.

Do the best that you know how to do
and you will move forward in your relationship
with less regrets and greater ease.

Write out five reasons why you fell in love with
your spouse to remind you of your true feelings.

Write out five reasons that you believe that your
mate fell in love with you to increase
your self-confidence.

Never break social plans with your spouse
unless it is an emergency.

Be willing to pay the price that it costs
to have a great marriage.

❧

Give your lover the freedom to express his:
anger
hurts
disappointments with you
frustrations

❧

Get rid of all of your self-doubts in order
to boost your own confidence level.

❧

Avoid the useless habit of worrying.

❧

When you argue, keep it from happening
in front of your children.

Things are never quite the same, somehow,
after you have to lie to a person.

Christopher Morley

Remember that when you are presenting your side
of an issue to your mate, the most powerful tool to
help your spouse see your side is the truth.

❧

Upgrade your tastes. Keep improving.

❧

To keep the passion alive:
pretend
play
dream
imagine

THE THREE BASIC ELEMENTS OF PROBLEM RESOLUTION FOR HAPPY MARRIAGES

1. Define it.
2. Solve it.
3. Forget it.

Take time out from each other's company
when you have been having the same argument
over and over without any resolution.

When you sow love, joy grows.

German proverb

Stand up for yourself.

Control your:
mouth
emotions
impulses

Watch your tone of voice
when you speak to your mate.

Understand that people are
more important than things.

Drop at least some of
your unrealistic expectations today.
Tomorrow work on dropping a few more.

Start over after a rough period.
Wipe the slate clean.

Stop keeping score.

Write out your mate's most important values
to get a better understanding of him.

Write out your most important values to
understand yourself a bit better.

What can you learn from these lists?
Share them with each other.

Find something positive in
every marital struggle.

Help your mate to feel important.

Develop a way about you that is always warm,
sincere, and friendly.

Dream huge, romantic dreams together
and then go for it!

Write your own eulogy from your
mate's point of view.

What did you learn from this exercise?

Stop making excuses for not having
the marriage of your dreams.

Only one life, that soon is past;
only what's done with love will last.

Author unknown

Consider recording a few of your conversations
with your spouse. What do you hear? How do you
feel about what is being said?

ᗑᓎ

Remember that you learn by listening. How often
do you spend time learning from your mate?

ᗑᓎ

Trust your instincts.

ᗑᓎ

Trust your mate's instincts.

Stay away from temptation.

That bears repeating.
Stay away from temptation!

Motivate your partner with:
love
gifts
affection
appreciation
cards
notes
words of gratitude

Say a prayer of thanks together
for your marriage tonight at bedtime.

Be not long away from home.

Homer

Keep in mind that privacy is an important
ingredient for love and romance.

Write out all of your beliefs about marriage.

Write out what you believe your mate
thinks about marriage.

Share these lists for some interesting conversation.

Rediscover your partner—
people are constantly changing.

Understand that when your mate is angry,
he is most likely feeling hurt
underneath that anger.

⟡

Break out of your ruts.

⟡

Look at your relationship from your mate's
point of view. Things can look very different
on that side of the fence.

⟡

Lighten up.

⟡

Stop complaining to friends and family about
your marriage. If you have a problem,
go directly to your mate.

Be careful what topics you choose to fight about.
Ask yourself if the situation really is important
enough to argue over.

Allow your partner to have financial freedom
within your agreed-upon budget.

Compliment your mate. Compliment your mate.
It is so important that I had to list it twice!

Be friends with your mate.

Long only for what you have.

André Gide

Invest your time in your marriage.

Have at least two or three close friends
other than your mate so that you won't be
overly dependent on your spouse.

Try hard to please your spouse
whenever you can.

Look through your wedding scrapbook together,
and reminisce about your feelings that day.

Keep in mind that you, to a very large degree,
create the life you are living.

CONVERSATIONS TO AVOID
WHEN TIRED OR STRESSED
• ———————————— •

partner's bad habits
finances
sexual dissatisfaction
leisure time activity complaints
your children's problems
chores

Just sit down and hold hands for five minutes
to reconnect after a long, hard day.

Love is an activity, a power of the soul.

Erich Fromm

Vow to be proactive instead of just reacting
to the events in your marriage.

Stop worrying about keeping up
with your neighbors.

No great thing is created suddenly.

Epictetus

Do the best that you can and then let it go.
Nobody can ask you for any more.

Be extra considerate to your mate
when he has problems at work.

How to Stay Calm
When a Marital Storm Hits

Breathe deeply.

Sit down.

Take a private moment or two for yourself.

Seek to understand the entire situation from
your mate's point of view.

Ask questions in a nonthreatening manner.

Listen intently.

Refrain from getting defensive.

Take some time apart from each other
to consider solutions.

Give the situation your full attention.

Draw up an action strategy together.

Try to say yes whenever you can
to your spouse.

Remember that your guardian angel
is always watching you.

Skip being competitive with your mate.
You are both on the same team.

Fight constructively.

Avoid things that upset or displease your love
if possible.

If there is no wind, row.

Latin proverb

Reevaluate your marriage as circumstances change
and as you and your mate change.

∾

Remember that all of your words, deeds,
and actions count toward making your
relationship better or worse.

Don't ask for things to be easier;
ask instead for you to be better.

Jim Rohn

Write out your own definition of a great romance.

∾

Never put your partner up on a pedestal
or she stops being your partner.

Cultivate shared interests.

Ask, ask, and keep on asking for what will make
you happy in your relationship. Make sure it is
within reason and it will benefit your mate, too.

During tough times, fake it till you make it,
as the saying goes.

Resolve to make your love life better
every day of your life.

Make it a habit to do what will make
your relationship successful.

Follow the Golden Rule. Treat your mate
like you want to be treated.

⁓

Pamper your mate when he is:
sick
tired
sad

⁓

Send a surprise gift.

⁓

Design special anniversary rings for
the two of you.

⁓

Only consider divorce as a final option.
Then try one last time to work things out.

Smile at each other throughout the day.

༄

Have separate checking accounts
to give each other more freedom.

༄

Invest your money wisely.

༄

Never use your circumstances as an excuse
for lack of trying.

THE BIGGEST ROMANCE KILLER

•───────•

Boredom

Overcome the circumstances
that are holding you back.

Love your mate in spite of her faults.

Write down all of your beliefs
about sex after marriage.
Share this list with your spouse to improve
your love life.

Listen with an open heart.

Stop giving ultimatums.

Fall in love all over again.

Count your joint blessings.

Remember that all marriages have their
highs and lows.

Work to find the right perspective
to have on your relationship issues.

Vow to be happy instead of always
having to be right.

Open your heart to receiving love.

Kiss—keep it simple,
when it comes to relationship matters.

Maintain a full life outside of your
relationship through:
religion
children
family
friends
career
pets
hobbies

Forgiveness means letting go of the past.

Gerald Jampolsky

Know that your mate wants your:
love
appreciation
respect

Pray for your mate.

⟋⟍

When disagreeing, always listen
to your mate's position first so you can fully
understand the whole situation.

⟋⟍

Force yourself to be upbeat about
the low points in the relationship.

⟋⟍

Stop testing your mate.

⟋⟍

Refrain from questioning your mate's love
and feelings for you.

⟋⟍

Make sure that your family treats your mate well.

Remember that good and bad habits are contagious.

෪

Show each other mutual respect even in the heart
of a major disagreement.

෪

Show an interest in your mate's:
career
hobbies
opinions
problems
family
friends
pets

෪

Be faithful.

෪

Flirt with each other over dinner tonight.

Never reward bad behavior from your spouse.
It will only encourage your mate to do
more of it in the future.

If your mate treats you badly, don't ignore the
problem. Work to solve the issue.

Love is shown best in little ways.

Linda Thomson

Wear red, the color of passion.

Say a lot more positive things
than negative things.

Mistrust destroys love, so try to have faith
in your marriage partner.

To live is good
To live vividly is better
To live vividly together is best.

Max Eastman

Show your appreciation every single time that
your mate does something nice for you.

Have lots of great couple friends.

Seek out friends who will enlarge your world
and make it more interesting and exciting.

Just because you are married, don't take
your single friends for granted. They can be
big supporters of your relationship.

Think of your relationship as a
masterpiece in progress.

HOW TO BE A GOOD LISTENER

Look your spouse in the eye.
Nod and show signs of agreement.
Ask questions.
Stay focused.
Have open body language.
Don't interrupt.
Concentrate on the conversation.

Remember that small steps
can have big payoffs.

Read your old love letters.

Some pursue happiness.
Others create it.

Author unknown

Never talk down to your mate.

To be a lover is not to make love,
but to find a new way to live.

Paul La Cour

Refrain from relying on your mate's friends
to be your only friends.

PRACTICE STRESS REDUCING
TECHNIQUES TOGETHER

meditation
yoga
exercise
eating healthy foods
less caffeine intake
less sugar consumption

Look at the role you choose to play
in your marriage.

Search for ways to create harmony.

LOVER—suitor, wooer, sweetheart

Refrain from taking your troubles out
on your mate.

All mankind loves a lover.

Ralph Waldo Emerson

Have a torrid affair with your mate
this weekend.

The smallest good deed is better
than the grandest intention.

Author unknown

Act out your favorite love scene from a movie.

Volunteer together to help others.

Sleep together till noon on Saturdays.

Decide on a budget that you both can live with.

Hide love notes for your mate in her:

car

office

clothes

Hire an artist to paint a wonderful painting
of the two of you.

Send cards.

Treat your in-laws with respect.

Cook your mate's favorite meal this weekend.

Do favors for one another.

Read love poetry to each other.

Be fun to be around.

Praise your mate in public.

Remember that the grass isn't really greener
on the other side.

Schedule a specific time for serious discussions
instead of letting frustrations out at a time
when you are extremely upset.

Keep in mind that no two people are alike.
Learn to appreciate your differences instead of
fighting against them.

Understand that some of the things that
irritate you most about your partner may be
caused by your own faults and insecurities
that you need to work on.

Never expect your mate to be able to
read your mind.

There are homes you run from
and homes you run to.

Laura Cunningham

Ask yourself each morning to write out three
things to improve your relationship for the day
and then choose one to try.

Share any relationship epiphanies you receive.
It will bring the two of you closer.

Be generous with your mate.

Learn to forgive and forget. It is a hard lesson
to learn, but it can make a huge difference
in the quality of your marriage.

Let go of all of your past mistakes.
Ask your partner to do the same.

Be tolerant.

Whisper kind and loving words to each other.

Get married all over again
in a flashy Las Vegas wedding.

Happily embrace your life together.

Hug good morning.

❧

Hug good-night.

Till I loved
I never lived.

Emily Dickinson

Write love letters to each other that are
filled with emotion and passion.

❧

Never go to bed angry with one another.

❧

Kiss and make up after every fight.

Try all good things at least once.

෧෮

Create your dream home together.

෧෮

Share your inheritance.

෧෮

Watch your credit card spending.

෧෮

Invent your own special holidays.

The man who never alters his opinions
is like standing water, and breeds
reptiles of the mind.

William Blake

Go to sleep with at least one body part touching
every single night.

Never invite your relatives to stay with you
until you have talked it over
with your spouse.

Save analysis for your shrink.
Don't overanalyze your relationship.

Write down how you and your mate spend
every minute during a typical twenty-four-
hour period. What are the patterns?
What changes can you both make to
improve your time together?

Never waste time worrying over what
other people think about your marriage.

Put everything in its place around your home
to keep things orderly and running smoothly.

Keep on plugging.

John Preston Downs

Overcome hatred with love.

Face troubles squarely.

Frame pictures of happy shared times together.

THE WORST RELATIONSHIP DANGERS

stonewalling/silent treatment
resentment
negativity
fear
jealousy
power struggles

Three is a crowd when it comes to
marital relationships. Don't allow friends or
family to come between the two of you.

Misery is a communicable disease.

Martha Graham

Nurture your:
mind
body
soul

∾

Invest in a quality retirement plan so that
growing old together will have a happy ending.

∾

Stay vibrant, alive, and loving no matter
how old you are.

∾

Understand the different passages that
different age groups experience, especially if
you and your mate are more than
ten years apart in age.

Have a gift budget that you both
can live with happily.

෧～෧

Always believe that you will make it
through your darkest hours.

෧～෧

Host fun family get-togethers for both
of your families.

෧～෧

Read newspaper and magazine articles
on relationship issues to learn
more coping skills.

෧～෧

When your marriage is struggling,
look for people who can give you the specific kind
of help that you both need.

Look at the bright side of each problem.
Play a game to see which one of you can come up
with the most creative ideas for determining
the bright side of the issue.

The key to success is to determine
your goal and then act as if it
were impossible to fail and it shall be!

Dorothea Brande

Vow to stay in love and work at it.

Keep *all* of your vows.

Spend a romantic weekend together
every few months.

Compose your own words to your
favorite love song.

Love is the active concern for the life
and the growth of that which we love.

Erich Fromm

Kiss hello.

⤳

Celebrate your mate's promotions in a big way.

⤳

Save together for a dream vacation.

⤳

Grow old together instead of growing apart.

Treat yourself to something luxurious
at a lovely lingerie shop.

Kiss in public when you feel so inclined.

Rent a romantic movie instead of the
usual blockbuster action picture.

E-mail each other throughout your workday.

Set aside fifteen minutes a day
to get in touch with one another.

Take dancing lessons together.

Make a list of ten things that you like about
your relationship and surprise
your spouse with it.

Browse a thesaurus for different romantic words
to use when speaking of your love.

Redecorate your bedroom to add a spark
to your love life.

Drop your grudge even if you know you are right.

Study what God has to say about marriage.

Splurge on an extravagant gift for your mate.

Share your lottery winnings.

Help keep yourself and your mate healthy
by eating a balanced diet.

Occasionally surprise your mate
with her favorite decadent treat.

There are two ways of meeting
difficulties. You alter the difficulties
or you can alter yourself to meet them.

Phyllis Bottome

Help keep your mate in good physical shape
by staying active together.

Refrain from gossiping about your partner.

Buy little tokens of love for each other.

Share your secrets.

If you have to say something negative
to your mate, say it:
privately
kindly
respectfully

A smile costs nothing
but its value is priceless.

Author unknown

How to Turn a Problem
into a Lesson in Love

• ——————— •

Decide what went wrong.

Understand the role you played in the
problem.

Determine what you did correctly.

Look for what you can learn from this
situation.

Take positive steps to resolve the issue for
good.

Get professional help if needed.

Look toward a happier future.

Husbands are like fires.
They go out when unattended.

Zsa Zsa Gabor

Send flowers and plants to express your love.

⟋⟍⟋

Work hard to raise your standard of living
to a comfortable level.

⟋⟍⟋

Share housekeeping chores.

⟋⟍⟋

Get over your romantic shyness.

⟋⟍⟋

Take a short vacation with no predetermined
destination in mind.

⟋⟍⟋

Meditate together in the wee small hours
of the morning.

Learn to speak French.
It is the language of lovers.

Refrain from using profanity.

Snuggle up on long airplane rides.

Love, and do what you like.

Saint Augustine

Be patient with your unromantic spouse.

Remember that manners matter.

Take your partner's feelings, dreams,
and goals to heart.

Make a detailed list of the issues that you feel
are causing stress in your relationship.
Now, begin trying to solve these, one at a time.

Regularly reinvent your:
relationship
hobbies
interests
activities

Just remember that opportunities are everywhere to
show your spouse just how much you care.

Become bigger than your troubles.

ᏀᏞ

Stand together against outside
influences and pressures.

ᏀᏞ

If you want a dream marriage, outperform
each other's expectations.

ᏀᏞ

Use some of your free time for some
high-quality self-improvement.

ᏀᏞ

Refrain from lending money to family or friends
unless you can afford not to get it back.

ᏀᏞ

Never interrupt while your mate is talking.

Things turn out best for people
who make the best out of the way
things turn out.

Author unknown

Keep in mind that just reading how to have
a great marriage isn't enough. You must
implement the necessary actions.

∽

The common thread of all bad relationships
is lack of effort on the part of one or both partners.

∽

Discover your mate's:
needs
wants
desires

Focus on the positive things about:
your mate
your relationship
marriage in general
love
romance

෴

Before you routinely answer your mate,
try to read between the lines of
what your mate just said.

෴

Listen more than you talk.

෴

Stop thinking that you have to have it all.

෴

Keep old flames in the past.

WHAT COUPLES REPORT
FIGHTING OVER THE MOST

• ———————— •

sex/intimacy
finances
chores
leisure time activities
children
in-laws

Have faith in God to see you both
through the tough times.

Learn to be silent.
Let your quiet mind listen and absorb.

Pythagoras

Quality is never an accident;
it is always the result of high intention,
sincere effort, intelligent direction,
and skillful execution; it represents
the wise choice of many alternatives.

John Ruskin

Pay attention to the little details of
your life together.

Make a list of the things you are doing
to prevent your relationship from becoming
a divorce statistic.
Keep doing these and more!

HOW TO HAVE
GREAT ANNIVERSARIES

• ———————— •

Make an effort to do something special to
celebrate the day.

Remember the occasion. Mark it on your
calendar.

Reminisce about your wedding and
honeymoon.

Play hooky together.

Send a romantic card.

Give a special gift.

Throw a party for the two of you.

Take a romantic trip.

Go out for breakfast, lunch, and dinner.

Spend the day in bed.

Decorate your house in a wedding theme
decor for the day.

Buy something special to wear when the
two of you go out to celebrate.

Send flowers.

Have a small replica of your wedding cake
for dessert.

Drink a toast to each other and your future.

Share your fondest memories as a married
couple.

Get married again.

Share your memories of your courtship.

Give an anniversary ring.

Share your dreams for the future.

Pray a prayer of gratitude for your
marriage.

Ask God to bless your marriage.

Say your vows privately to each other.

Return to your honeymoon hotel.

Don't allow your parents to interfere
in your marriage.

∽

Focus more on solutions than
on the cause of your troubles.

The opposite of love is not hate,
it's indifference.

Elie Wiesel

Celebrate your mate's birthday in a
special way every year.

∽

Drop the nasty habit of
trying to improve your mate.

Throw fun parties together.

Kiss good-night every single night of the year.

Help your partner to stay out of debt
if he loves to shop.

Develop friendships with spiritual people.

Snuggle during the cold winter nights
in front of a roaring fire.

Buy an antique quilt for cuddling.

If it won't get your mate in trouble,
send your mate romantic faxes.

∽

Refrain from being judgmental.

∽

Send candy—you know, sweets to the sweets.

∽

Live without television for an entire month
to get reacquainted.

∽

Splurge on great evenings out
on the town together.

∽

Take a week off from work at Christmastime
and share the magic of the season.

It is very easy to forgive others
their mistakes; it takes more grit to
forgive them for having witnessed
your own.

Jessamyn West

Hold hands during thunderstorms
to feel some real electricity.

Wake up ten minutes early just to snuggle.

Accept yourself. Acceptance is contagious.

Overlook the aging process.

Share your romantic fantasies.

෯∾෨

Turn your hobby into a wonderful joint career.

෯∾෨

Keep a journal of your positive feelings about:
your mate
your marriage
love
romance

෯∾෨

Rent a romantic cabin in the woods for weekend
getaways.

෯∾෨

Give her a new engagement ring
that will knock her socks off!

Cultivate a very good sense of humor about:
yourself
your mate
your sex life
marriage
the opposite sex

Help out your in-laws in times of trouble.

Just be kind.

Refrain from appearing stubborn
even when you know you are right.

Keep in mind that no marriage
is without its problems.

Want to stop the chore war? Just make a chart
to show who should do which job.

❦

Play Truth or Dare to break out of your
"we don't have anything new to talk about" rut.

❦

Attend lots of romantic concerts.

❦

Kiss all night long.

❦

Celebrate all holidays together.

❦

Buy a hammock for your backyard so you can
share it under the stars.

Dress for Halloween parties
as a great romantic couple.

Even the most ordinary life
is a mystery if you look close enough.

Kennedy Fraser

Persevere when problems arise!

∾

Love your mate even in the darkest times.

∾

Support your mate's favorite charity by:
giving of your time
making a cash donation

Understand that these big changes will bring
periods of adjustments for you and your spouse.
Plan on steps you can take to make things easier
for both of you during:

the birth of a child

promotions

moves

health issues

the loss of a parent

the loss of a job

Inspire your mate to do his best.

Cooking is like love. It should be
entered into with abandon or not at all.

Harriet Van Horne

Eliminate all unnecessary activities
that take away time from each other.

Keep a pen and paper by your bed at night
to write down great ideas that come to you in the
middle of the night for improving your marriage.

Save time by doing two or three things at once to
free up more time for fun with your mate.

Clean out your own bad habits just like you
clean out your closet.

Break out of your comfort zone
to liven things up a bit.

Nothing ever happens in your life
unless you create the space for it
to happen in.

James McCay

Look at all marriage challenges
from a long-term perspective.

∽

Make some of the gifts you give to your mate
to add a touch of love.

∽

Start early in your marriage to divorce-proof it.

∽

Ask your mate for her ideas about
improving your relationship.

THE MOST POPULAR ANNIVERSARY GIFTS

• ———————— •

jewelry

trips to romantic destinations

flowers and candy

lingerie

champagne

books and games

artwork

Remember that you can't fix everything about your marriage at one time. Pick a specific area to work on, and when you are happy in that area, move to the next area for improvement.

Decide how to best spend your time
with your mate.

Never argue with your mate right before bedtime.

Try to adjust the two of you to your different:
biological clocks
work styles
time frames
personalities
stress levels
sleep requirements

Keep your mate informed about your
social calendar and work schedule.

Do a marriage analysis as if you were a social
worker looking objectively at your relationship.
What do you see?

Eliminate unwanted noise in your bedroom by:
playing CDs
listening to nature tapes
getting a ceiling fan

Refrain from watching television in bed.

Time eases all things.

Sophocles

Take naps to feel rested so that you can enjoy the evenings together.

Unwind before going to bed.

Spend less time acquiring things and more time enjoying your mate.

Learn to be satisfied and grateful for what you have.

Consider moving to a smaller home to save money and to spend less time in maintaining it, which could make things easier for you and your mate.

Do what you can, with what you have,
where you are.

Theodore Roosevelt

If you are seriously in debt, seek professional help
to get out of your financial straits.

Have at least one weekend a month
that is chore free for the entire family.

Stop trying to change your in-laws.

Go on a marriage enrichment retreat.

Work to uncomplicate your expectations.

∽

Become more self-sufficient.

∽

Celebrate the nice, ordinary rituals
of your daily life together.

How to Say No to Your Spouse

• ———— •

Be diplomatic.
Be firm.
Present your side in an upbeat manner.
Be loving.
Give a specific reason why you are turning
    down your mate.
Expect some possible negative feedback.

Put your mate's number in the
number-one spot on your speed dial.

To make sure that you spend plenty of time
with your mate, set up planned appointments
to get together.

There are two rules for
achieving anything.
Rule Number One: Get started.
Rule Number Two: Keep going.

Howard Hunt

Practice new desired behaviors.

Tackle tough conversations and decisions during
high energy periods in your day.

Keep a chart of your time spent together
for a month. How much time do
the two of you really spend
enjoying each other's company?

The only hope of preserving what is best
lies in the practice of an
immense charity, a wide tolerance,
a sincere respect for opinions
that are not ours.

P. G. Hamerton

Never invest more effort, time, or focus than
a specific marital problem warrants.

Read the latest best-sellers on relationships.

Never assume that you know what your mate
is thinking. Check it out by asking questions.

Paraphrase what your mate says to you
to make sure that you fully grasp what
is being expressed.

Commute together to work.

Think before you speak.

Ask lots of open-ended questions.

Anticipate some resistance
when you make changes in:
yourself
your relationship
your routine
your home
your feelings

Take dates with your mate seriously.

Remember that you can't control everything.

Read a book on stress management and share
what you learn with your partner.

Use questions to keep conversations on track,
interesting, and revealing.

There's a price for every prize.
Everyone wants the prize, but no one
wants to pay the price.

Robert Schuller

Consider the costs and benefits of deciding to work
or not work on your relationship.

Refrain from being a perfectionist.

Never wait for the romantic or loving mood to
strike you—just act!

Commit yourself today to change your marriage
for the better even if you have been married
for years and you are happy.

❦

Make one radical but positive change this week.

❦

Stop demanding things.

❦

Put down your romantic novels and live out some
of your romantic fantasies with your spouse.

The more you do of what
you are doing, the more you'll get
of what you are getting.

Greek proverb

Look for God's hand in your relationship.

Think of your marriage as an affair.

TWO OF THE MOST IMPORTANT WORDS
TO MAKE A MARRIAGE LAST:
"FORGIVE ME."

Question your parents about how they
solved their troubles.

A man becomes like the people
he lives with.

Hindu proverb

TRAVEL TIPS FOR SECOND HONEYMOONS

• ———————— •

Set goals for your trip.

Plan carefully. This is a vacation that you
will remember forever.

Vote on activities. Refrain from
overscheduling.

Pace yourselves.

Be careful what you eat and drink.

Travel light.

Leave your children at home.

Leave work behind.

Pack clothes that can take you from day
into evening.

Have a good trip checklist.

Confirm hotel and airline reservations
before you leave home.

Expect travel delays.

Take travel medicine along.

Pack a gift for your mate.
Take along your most romantic attitude.
Relax and fall in love all over again.
Leave your itinerary at home with family
and friends.

Ask your mate about possible areas of concern
to your mate to explore hot spots before
major troubles set in.

Reward positive changes in:
yourself
your mate
your relationship

When good things happen,
share credit with your spouse.

Turn your stumbling blocks
into stepping stones.

Author unknown

Accept graciously all of the compliments you
receive from your love.

Share your deepest convictions and beliefs with
your mate.

Pamper yourselves tonight.

Expect your mate to treat you with
dignity and respect.

Play detective to learn whom your mate
really is deep inside.

Build an atmosphere of trust in your home.

Be the right partner for your mate.

Refrain from using guilt to get what you want.

Stop manipulating your spouse.

Enlist the help of your family when you
are encountering a crisis in your relationship.

Write out the five most important components
of your romantic style.

Write out the five most important components
of your mate's romantic style.

What similarities do you notice in your lists?
What differences do you see? Now share these
lists with your mate.

Remember that all relationships hit plateaus.

Speak of love, joy, and peace.

Turn the other cheek.

Remember, you promised for 24/7.

Keep growing together because the moment
that you start growing apart, you begin
to lose each other.

Think balance.

Remember that a marital crisis
is simply a cry to become better.

Pull together when a friend's marriage fails.
This can be a really tricky time for marriages.

Enjoy the simple things in life together.

Understand your:
motives
feelings
actions

❦

Cling to your mate if you suffer
a miscarriage or loss of a child.

❦

Remember: If you look for faults in your mate,
yourself, or your relationship, you will
surely find them.

❦

Ask yourself if you focus more
on your joys or sorrows.

❦

Develop a high level of tolerance.

Monitor your voice and speech pattern.
Do you sound like a lover or a tyrant?

Imagine that you are your mate for the next five
minutes. Write out the first five things that you
think would pop into his mind about you.

Sleep on this idea and write out five more things
about yourself from your mate's point of view in
the morning. What have you learned?

Tread cautiously when heading
into midlife-crisis time.

There are no shortcuts on the road
to a great marriage.

Never settle for less than the best marriage that
the two of you are capable of achieving.

I would give up all my fame
and all my art if there were one woman
who cared whether or not I came home
late for dinner.

Ivan Turgenev

Remember that your wedding day should be
the beginning of your love story, not the end.

❧

MARRIAGE—matrimony, union, wedlock, nuptial tie.

❧

Be tender with your mate's feelings.

Learn to enjoy solitude so your times together
will be enhanced.

∽

Give your love without strings attached.

SOLVE YOUR MARITAL PROBLEMS
FOR THE SAKE OF YOUR:

physical health
emotional health
spiritual health
children
mate's health and happiness
wedding vows

Massage each other's backs and feet
to relieve tension.

Hurt not others with that which
pains yourself.

Udana—Varga

Stop comparing your sex life with others'.

Refrain from comparing your current sex life
to a different period in your relationship.

Remember that marriage is a lifetime contract.

Keep in mind that when people are on their
deathbeds, they never wish that they had spent
more time at work.

Allow your mate to be herself.

Thou shall not commit adultery.

God

Surround yourselves with beautiful things.

Don't let jealousy strike you
when your mate gets a big promotion.

Pray for your mate's recovery when he is sick.

Modify your marriage goals as needed.

Remember if you are having marital problems
that you aren't the first couple and you won't be
the last couple to have troubles. Relax.

Commit your marriage goals for the next six
months to paper and place them where you will see
them at least once a day.

Refrain from spreading yourself too thin.

When you are making changes, do not give up or
be disheartened if things don't improve right away.
Some things just take time. Remember it took you
awhile to get where you are and it may take awhile
to get to where you want to be.

When you blame others, you give up the
power to change.

Author unknown

Give yourselves some freedom by:
being more spontaneous
straight shooting all issues
being open to change
remaining open to love

Enjoy your wedding gifts.
Get them out of the closet and use them.

Try not to bring work home from the office.

FORGIVENESS 101, OR HOW TO FORGIVE

•———————•

Choose forgiveness over holding on to the
hurt.

Forgive yourself for any mistakes you have
made.

Ask for forgiveness from your partner.

Pray.

Forget the incident and let it go.

Never hurt your mate's feelings on purpose.

Create an exciting, romantic diversion in
your relationship tonight.

Remember variety is the spice of life.

Understand that we all carry hurts
from our childhood. Try to heal yours
before they hurt your marriage.

When your love is away on a business trip,
pack your photo in his suitcase.

Make a collage of your ideal:
home
schedule
wardrobe
leisure time activities

Expect your times together to be wonderful.

Just for tonight, pretend to be other people
and see what happens.

❧

Create more romance for yourselves by planting
a beautiful rose garden.

❧

Attend romantic plays.

❧

Vow to be a huge positive influence
on your mate's life.

❧

Stay awake together to see the sunrise.

❧

Collect souvenirs from all of the concerts, trips,
plays, and special events that the two of you go to.

Everyone must row
with the oars they have.

English proverb

KEEP YOUR THOUGHTS . . .

●───────────●

positive

fresh

goal-oriented

playful

romantic

humorous

sexy

Your relationship will be better because of it.

Live without regrets.

After a stressful day, take a bubble bath
or long, hot shower to unwind
before spending time with your mate.

❧

Say no when it feels right.

❧

Always give your mate the benefit of the doubt.

❧

Do things differently around the house to
liven things up a bit.

❧

Notice the attention and affection
that your mate sends your way.

❧

Have faith in your marriage.

TRADITIONAL ANNIVERSARY GIFT SUGGESTIONS

• ──────── •

First—paper
Fifth—wood
Tenth—tin
Fifteenth—crystal
Twentieth—china
Twenty-fifth—silver
Thirtieth—pearl
Fortieth—ruby
Fiftieth—gold

Propel yourself forward one step at a time.

Get a pet. Pet owners report a higher
satisfaction level in their marriages.

A cheerful heart causes good healing.

Proverbs 17:22

Break your big marriage goals down
into workable, little steps.

The great thing in this world is not
so much where we stand as in what
direction we are moving.

Oliver Wendell Holmes

Ask yourself if you are easy to live with.
Why or why not?

MAINTAIN YOUR HEALTH

• ———————— •

Get enough sleep.

Drink plenty of water.

Take your vitamins.

Exercise.

Eat only healthy foods.

Don't smoke.

Keep your stress level low.

Remember it is harder to be romantic

when you aren't feeling well.

A tiny change today brings us a
dramatically different tomorrow.

To be desirable, be happy and fulfilled
outside of your marriage.

There are grand rewards for those
who pick the high roads.

Richard Bach

Write down the important moments between
the two of you that have changed things
for better or worse.

What can you learn from this list to help
your marriage? How can you use this information
to improve the quality of your relationship?

Get to work on this starting now!

Close your eyes and take a mental mini-vacation
during stressful moments.

LOVING SPOUSES ARE . . .

•————————•

open
flexible
helpful
trustworthy
kind
generous
honest
warm

Do you possess these qualities?

Never put yourself down
in order to build up your mate.

Keep in mind that many marriages are stronger
after a crisis than before the trouble hit.

Break free from any unhealthy influences
of your parents and in-laws.

Do not blame anybody for your
mistakes and failures.

Bernard M. Baruch

Ask yourself what you can do today
to improve your:
marriage
home life
sex life
happiness level

Keep in mind that many marriages are stronger
after a crisis than before the trouble hit.

What character flaws do you need to heal
that are hurting your marriage?

What is keeping you from healing them?
Ask for your mate's help.

Start the healing process today!

Begin anew every day.

The long run is possible
only if we consistently take care
of the short run.

William H. Calvin

Destroy your prenuptial agreement.

⁓

Have a "We are going to be together forever" celebration and make it a night to end all nights.

⁓

Keep in mind that love is contagious.

You live that you may learn to love.
You love that you may learn to live.
No other lesson is required.

Mirdad

Lean on each other when one of you experiences the death of a parent.

If you can't reach a solution to a specific problem,
write out possible solutions and exchange
your lists. Keep doing this until you can both
agree on a way to make things right.

Visualize what you want for your marriage
in the future instead of dwelling on
your present situation.

For a little romantic adventure, take a
hot-air balloon ride together.

Ask your friends for their best marital advice.

Take an extended vacation together.

Whisper romantic sayings in each other's ears
tonight by candlelight.

Snuggle all night long.

Take lots of horse-drawn carriage rides.

Spend some winter weekends at
romantic ski lodges.

Write down all of your beliefs about love.
Share these with your mate.

Make love in lots of romantic locations.

Check out self-help books, romance novels,
and poetry books from your library to keep you
in a romantic and happy frame of mind.

Write a couple's mission statement describing
the relationship that you both want to have.
Keep it in a place where you'll see it often.

Read the biographies of happily married people.

Have a fireplace in your bedroom.

Sing love songs to each other.

Dance at home together.

Talk to widows and widowers to regain a sense of
appreciation about having your spouse in your life.

෧～෨

Talk to your single friends to also gain a sense of
appreciation about being married.

෧～෨

Keep your sense of humor when you:
get irritated with your mate
have big issues to resolve
in your relationship

෧～෨

Use mistletoe on your mate and
don't just save it for late December.

෧～෨

Refrain from yelling at your mate
when you are angry.

Mellow out with a romantic CD and fall
in love all over again.

∽

Put fun ads that express your love in the classifieds
for each other to find.

∽

Dine out at romantic restaurants.

∽

Stay in the honeymoon suite when you travel.

∽

Help each other grieve when you lose
a beloved family pet.

∽

Stay close to each other during the
transition period following a move.

You cannot change anyone
except yourself. After you have become
an example, you can inspire others
to change themselves.

Peace Pilgrim

Call home when you are away on business trips.

❧

Take romantic cruises.

❧

Hold hands in public.

❧

Be 100 percent committed to making your
marriage a lifetime affair of the heart.

Say "I love you" every day.

Get a massage for two.

Attend lots of weddings together.

Flirt only with each other.

Wink at each other from across a crowded room.

Happily attend your mate's office functions.

Vow to jump-start your sex life.

Form a book club with other couples to discuss relationship books.

∼

Have some meals at home catered to make them special and romantic.

THROW A GREAT SPOUSE APPRECIATION PARTY

•—————————•

Surprise your mate.

Hold it in a romantic setting.

Serve delicious food.

Videotape it for some special memories.

Invite your mate's favorite people.

Decorate in a style that would suit your
        mate's taste.

Buy your mate something special to wear
        to the party.

Buy a lock for your bedroom door
if you have children.

Get married all over again in grand style—
go to Paris.

Write down ten things that would make
you feel loved by your mate.
Share this list with your mate.
Now, get your mate to do the same.

If you don't have anything nice to say,
shut your mouth!

Author unknown

Throw a party for all of the people who were in your wedding.

❦

Write out a two-week plan of dates, gestures, and fun ideas to improve your marriage.

❦

If you want things to improve, make better, smarter decisions about your relationship than you have in the past.

❦

Make sure that your mate's expectations are realistic.

❦

Cling to each other when a close friend dies.

Most folks are about as happy as they
make up their minds to be.

Abraham Lincoln

CHECK YOUR EMOTIONAL HEALTH

•————————•

How does your body feel? Are you tense or
relaxed?

Are you happy?

Are your healthy?

Do you feel optimistic about your future?

Do you sleep well?

If you aren't emotionally healthy, your
marriage will suffer.

Affirm your mate.

Keep in mind that strong people ask for help.

TWO OF THE MOST IMPORTANT
WORDS TO BRING RESOLUTION:
"I'M SORRY"

Improve the nurturing side of your personality.

Love and you shall be loved.

Ralph Waldo Emerson

If competition gets in your way,
stay away from competitive games and sports
with your mate.

Remember that you cannot control
your mate's emotions, feelings, or actions.

Practice self-restraint.

Refrain from fishing for compliments.

Ask for the moon, reach for the stars.
At least you'll be flying!

Enjoy the stage of life that you are in.

Stop procrastinating.

Don't rationalize your problems away.

Indulge each other's whims.

Make home movies so you can relive
the happy times.

Write down all your beliefs about the opposite sex.

What insights do you have from looking
at your list?

To love is to stop comparing.

Author unknown

HOW TO BE YOUR BEST

• ———————— •

Talk about your success.

Focus on your good points.

Surround yourself with positive,
    supportive friends.

View your mistakes as learning tools.

Forgive yourself for not being perfect.

Imagine or visualize the life you want for
    yourself.

Learn new skills.

Start new projects or hobbies.

Take action instead of just dreaming.

Exercise.

Dress your best.

Learn relaxation techniques.

Get a makeover.

Have a spiritual foundation.

Encourage your mate to
seek professional help if he:
drinks too much
gambles excessively
is physically or emotionally abusive
can't hold a job
is depressed

❧

Show off your best side today.

Consider that this day
will never dawn again.

Dante

Say no to invitations that don't sound good,
fun, or healthy for your relationship.

Give back to your:
mate
friends
family
community
self
church

As soon as you trust yourself,
you will know how to live.

Goethe

Build bridges instead of walls.

Try to see your mate in environments
where he shines.

The purest and most thoughtful minds are
those which love colors the most.

John Ruskin

Pray for loving feelings toward your spouse.

What were the main reasons that
you wanted to get married?

What were the main reasons that you
wanted to marry your spouse?

Share these reasons with your mate.

Get a comfortable mattress.

HAVE A YEAR'S WORTH OF ROMANCE

• ———————— •

New Year's Day

Exchange romantic gifts at sunrise.

Breakfast in bed together.

Make resolutions of fun and romance.

Dinner out at a five-star restaurant.

Romantic trip to begin the new year.

Valentine's Day

Go on a romantic escape.

Take the day off from work together.

Have dinner at the restaurant of your first
dinner together.

Exchange love letters.

Read your old love letters.

Use the standards—flowers, candy, and
cards—to add romance.

Easter

Hide a piece of jewelry in an egg.

Go on a spring break.

Rededicate yourselves to falling in love
    during this beautiful time of the year.

May Day

Send a bouquet.

Spend the day on a romantic picnic.

Stroll in a beautiful garden.

Mother's Day/Father's Day

Celebrate the joy of being parents together.

Memorial Day, Fourth of July, and Labor Day

Take romantic getaway weekend trips.

Go on long and lazy picnics together.

Share fun-in-the-sun times.

Entertain together.

Dance under the stars.

Thanksgiving

Cook together.

Count your blessings in front of a roaring
fire.

Entertain your loved ones together.

Go to a great ballgame and snuggle under a
blanket to keep warm.

Christmas

Shop together.

Attend parties.

Go caroling.

Decorate your home.

Attend religious ceremonies.

Entertain.

Bake holiday treats.

New Year's Eve
Stay home and enjoy this special time
    alone.
Party-hop together.
Set goals for your future together.
Dress up to impress each other.
Forgive past transgressions.
Kiss at midnight.

We must be willing to get rid
of the life we've planned, so as to
have the life that is waiting for us.

Joseph Campbell

Be on time. This is so simple, but it can
make a huge difference.

To find something funny one only has
to look at themselves.

Jay Ward

Have strong values.

∽

Dress in complementary styles of clothing to feel
more comfortable around each other when you go
out on the town.

∽

Stretch yourself by:
reading
studying
observing
learning new things

Seek to understand:
yourself
your mate

∽

Your marriage goals need to be:
explicit
measurable
worthwhile

∽

Pray for guidance.

∽

Play "your song" often.

∽

Remember that you are never alone,
even if you are feeling lonely in your marriage,
for God is always with you.

Reward yourself for the good efforts you make
on behalf of your relationship. Give yourself a:
little pampering
mental pat on the back
gift

❧

Never expect your mate to change if you aren't
willing to change some things about yourself.

❧

Keep in mind that there is joy in giving
and in receiving.

Most people look at what is
and never see what can be.

Albert Einstein

THE BASICS OF
MARITAL PROBLEM SOLVING

•————————•

Define what is bothering you.

Define what is bothering your mate.

Make sure that you both understand these
issues.

Brainstorm solutions—the more the merrier.

Evaluate the solutions.

Pick the best option and try it out.

If it works, good for you. If not, pick
another possible solution and try it out.
Keep trying solutions until you get one
that does the job.

If the problem doesn't get solved after
trying, seek help from a trained
professional.

Remind yourself about what is really important in
your life to keep the proper perspective on things.

❦

Make a collage of your happy times together and
hang it where you both can see it every day.

❦

Start changing your negative expectations
into positive ones beginning right now.

❦

Ask your minister to bless your home.

❦

Be fair.

❦

Try aromatherapy to relieve tensions.

BEWARE OF THE FOLLOWING

• ———————— •

infidelity
dishonesty
selfishness
poor grooming habits
envy
lack of help around the house
jealousy

Place flowers and plants around your home
to cheer things up a bit.

Notice one new thing about your mate
or his behavior today.

Have faith in your partner.

❧

Allow your mate to live her life her way.

❧

Side with your mate in family squabbles
whenever you possibly can.

True friendship comes when silence
between two people is comfortable.

Dave Gentry

After each bump in the road to true marital bliss,
ask yourself what you have gained
from the experience.

ASK YOURSELF

• ——————— •

Am I fun?
Am I kind?
Am I romantic?
Am I sexy?
Am I thoughtful?
Am I loyal and faithful?
Am I honest all the time or just when it
   suits my purpose?
Am I polite?
Would I want to be married to someone
   like me?

Whatever there is that ought to be,
can be.

James Rause

Brag about your mate to others in front of him.

Have special dinners at home without the kids.

Giggle under the covers together.

Play footsie.

Stay up together after the kids go to bed.

Dance, walk, and laugh in the rain together.

Get a "Do not disturb" sign for your bedroom door.

Savor the special moments when you feel
really connected to each other.

∽

Have pet names for each other that are sweet
and romantic.

If you aren't going all the way,
why go at all?

Joe Namath

When you need advice,
ask your mate for his input.

∽

Refrain from lecturing your mate.

Make a collage together of your dream home.

What did you learn about your mate's taste
from this exercise?

Remember that it isn't enough to just love
your mate. You must show it.

Spend time with your mate. This sounds so basic,
but many couples talk to each other less than
five minutes per day.

Try to understand the important difference
between acting and reacting to marital stresses.

TIMES TO GIVE GIFTS TO YOUR MATE

• ——————— •

birthday

anniversaries

after a romantic evening

during a special night out on the town

when your partner is ill

when your mate gets a big promotion

when you need a bribe to get out of trouble

for made-up holidays

during stressful times to say that you care

just because!

The rules of successful marriage are not taught
in schools, so seek out different avenues to
learn how to be happily married.

Handle your marriage with tender loving care.

Spend time thinking about God's plan
for your relationship.

CREATE THE ROMANTIC BEDROOM OF YOUR DREAMS

•————————•

The bed

Have beautiful, clean sheets.

Have a lovely bedspread or comforter that
looks great in your room.

Use comfortable pillows for sleeping and
lots of decorative pillows for style.

Have a quilt or afghan at the foot of the bed
for added coziness and comfort.

The windows

Use heavy drapes or blinds for privacy and
to keep the room dark.

Accessories

Have lots of candles.

Install a dimmer switch on your overhead
light.

Have a CD player in the room loaded with
romantic music.

Place fresh flowers on the nightstand.

Keep fruit or chocolates on the nightstand.

Use wonderful air freshener.

Love casts out fear; but, conversely,
fear casts out love.

Aldous Huxley

Understand that your mate will not always
say yes to your requests.

Touch often, both physically and emotionally.

Kindly bring to light all of the issues
that need to be fixed.

Honor your differences and similarities.

Laugh with your mate, not at her.

Send little love notes when you don't have time
to write a letter.

Ask your minister to bless your marriage.

If we cannot adjust our differences
peacefully we are less than human.

Frank Herbert

Refrain from counting on your spouse to play too
many different roles in your life. Spread out those
roles among other friends and family members.

Use your talents to bring more joy
to your relationship.

Ask yourself if your mate is playing the role of
your:
best friend
lover
business partner
financial partner
sports partner
Are you comfortable with the way things are?

Examine your friendships with the opposite sex.
What are you looking for in these relationships?
Are you looking for the missing piece of
your relationship with your spouse?

Take care to get what you like or
you will be forced to like what you get.

George Bernard Shaw

Whenever you reach a marital goal, set a new one.

❧

Stay in the present moment:
Live there.
Love there.
Make changes there.

❧

Occupy your mind with calming,
helpful thoughts when problems hit.

❧

Create a marriage time line for implementing
changes and for reaching goals together.

❧

Figure out for yourself the type of mate
that you want and want to be.

Use an alternative term for your mate.
The word *spouse* can sound rather boring.
Consider:
lover
soul mate
helper
life mate
husband or wife
life partner

Write out ten things that seem important to you
about your parents' marriage.

Ask your mate to do the same for his memories
regarding his parents' marriage.

What insights can the two of you gain from what
you now realize about your parents' marriages?

It is not fair to ask of others what you
are not willing to do yourself.

—Eleanor Roosevelt

Consider giving some of these gifts to your mate:
your time
your help
teaching your mate new skills
pure luxury
your help in times of need

Much unhappiness results from
our inability to remember the nice things
that happen to us.

W. N. Rieger

PEOPLE EVERY MARRIED COUPLE SHOULD KNOW

• ———————— •

your banker
a good lawyer
a fine accountant
an excellent stockbroker
a wise financial planner

Don't wait for special occasions
to give your best gifts.

It is a funny thing about life. If you
refuse to settle for anything less than the
best, that's what it will give you.

W. Somerset Maugham

Explore the many different styles of marriage
that were part of your family tree.
What patterns are there?

Explore the different styles of marriages in your
mate's family tree. What are the patterns found
there? Are your families' styles compatible?

Create a help jar that consists of coupons for:
favors
chores of choice
backrubs
footrubs

One has a right to criticize,
who has a heart to help.

Abraham Lincoln

BUILD A SPIRITUAL FOUNDATION FOR YOUR MARRIAGE BY . . .

• ─────── •

attending religious services together

sharing your beliefs with one another

praying together at least once a day

reading the Bible together

attending Sunday school together

singing hymns together

celebrating all religious holidays with each
    other

sharing your faith together with your children

dedicating your relationship to God

Confront your fears.

Enjoy each day as if it were your last.

Write out the names of five couples
whose marriages you admire.

Now write out the qualities that make
these marriages so special.

What can you do to instill some of these
qualities in your own marriage?

Enjoy each day as if it were your first
with your mate.

A man should always consider . . .
how much more unhappy he might be
than he is.

Joseph Addison

Remember that your mate will love you to the
degree that you can love yourself.

Keep a record of the gifts that you give to your
mate and make little notations about any gifts that
were especially well received so that you might give
a similar type of gift in the future.

The things that hurt, instruct.

Ben Franklin

Have a marriage mentor who you can talk to on a
regular basis about relationship issues.

Ask your minister for marital advice.

Take a midweek vacation to jump-start
your weekend fun.

CREATE THE ROMANTIC BATHROOM OF YOUR DREAMS

•————————•

Have it spotlessly clean.

Use plush towels.

Have fragrant soaps.

Have matching robes.

Get music piped in.

Design his and her closets.

Have his and her dressing areas.

Get a huge whirlpool tub.

Hang beautiful pictures on the walls that
    have a romantic feel.

Meet for lots of lunches.

A great deal depends upon the thought
patterns we choose and on the persistence
with which we affirm them.

Piero Ferrucci

MAKE SURE THAT YOU KNOW HIS SIZES

• ——————— •

shirt
slacks
jacket
sweater
coat

MAKE SURE THAT YOU KNOW HIS FAVORITES

• ——————— •

color
store
cologne

The creation of something new is not accomplished by the intellect but by the play instinct acting from inner necessity. The creative mind plays with the objects it loves.

Carl G. Jung

Join a marriage-enrichment group.
They are springing up all over the country.

Jealousy is a way of getting rid of everything you are afraid of losing.

Author unknown

Exercise together after work to work off stress.

FINANCES FOR MARRIED COUPLES 101
(BECAUSE IT IS SUCH A HOT SPOT!)

• ———————— •

Buy financial planning software.

Save your tax returns.

Have a will.

Make a list of all of your assets and keep it
   in a safe place.

Organize all of your financial papers.

Take photos of your valuables and keep
   them in your safety deposit box.

Save 10 percent or more of your income.

Give 10 percent or more of your income to
   your church.

If you shop on-line, buy from only secure
   Web sites.

Keep your receipts for big-ticket items.

Make a list of your debts.

Form a plan to pay them off.

Prioritize your financial goals.

Consider keeping separate charge accounts for personal use.

Set high standards for yourselves.

Write down all of your expenses for a month to see where your money really goes.

Pay off your credit card debt.

Attend financial workshops and seminars together.

Study books, magazines, and newspaper articles on becoming financially savvy.

Decide what constitutes a major purchase.

Think about major purchases for at least a week before taking the buying plunge.

Never buy a home that costs more than twice your joint incomes.

Have at least three or four months' income stashed away in case of an emergency.

Plan together for your children's education.

Have a joint IRA account.

Invest in your company's 401K programs.

Get a fifteen-year mortgage instead of a
thirty-year.

IF YOU DECIDE TO USE CREDIT CARDS

•————————•

Shop for the lowest interest rates.

Get one that doesn't require you to pay a
user fee.

Carry one that gives back bonuses.

Never get a cash advance on it.

The interest rates are sky high!

Pay the balance at the end of each month.

If you get into trouble, seek help early.

Write out your top five financial goals as a couple.
Work at accomplishing these, one at a time.

MAKE SURE YOU KNOW HER SIZES

• —————— •

dress
slacks
blouse
blazer
sweater
gown/robe
coat

MAKE SURE YOU KNOW HER FAVORITES

• —————— •

color
store
perfume

The past and the future are the
gift wrapping for the present.

Jerry Downs

Get interested in the specifics
of your spouse's life:
hobbies
family
friends
charities
religious activities

Live as you will wish to have lived
when you are dying.

Christian Furchtegott Gellert

Move sex from being a nighttime-only activity
to an anytime activity.

Don't ignore your sex life.

Make love in different ways to keep sex
from becoming routine.

Spend lots of time alone with one another.

Never mistake intimacy for sex.

Create the home life that you and your mate
always wanted to have when you were young.

SET THE STAGE FOR GREAT SEX

• ──────────── •

Connect beforehand with intimate
conversation.

Play romantic music in the background.

Open a bottle of fine wine.

Dim the lights.

Whisper sweet nothings.

Surprise your love with a gift.

Call your spouse the next day to say that
last night was fabulous.

He that is discontented in one place
will seldom be happy in another.

Aesop

Congratulate yourselves when you have
a problem and seek help.

∽

Feel the pride of not being a divorce statistic.

∽

Take lots of strolls in nature
because they are:
private
beautiful
soothing
a great way to reconnect

∽

Try to always side with your mate
against negative influences in his world.

∽

Enforce a no-put-down policy in your home.

When you learn to live for others,
they will live for you.

Paramahansa Yogananda

REASONS MARRIED MEN
SHOULD STAY MARRIED

• —————————— •

They are healthier than single men.
They live longer than their single
 counterparts.
Studies show they are happier than their
 single friends.

Appreciate the fact that you can balance each
other's quirks. You can be the ying to his yang.

Have lots of quiet time in your home:
Turn off the television when you
aren't really watching.
Lower the volume on radios and CD players.
Calm the barking dog.
Quiet the kids.

❧

Make sure your children know
that you love each other.

❧

Courtship and dating should not end on your
wedding day. Keep busy wooing your mate.

❧

Build the marriage that you both dream of and
not the one that you believe you are supposed
to have based on your age, kids' opinion,
or your parents' influences.

Dress to impress your mate for a week or two.
See what happens.

Before you consider divorce, think of
your children. The latest research studies
suggest that you *should* stay married
for the sake of your kids.

Never argue in the bedroom and
especially not in bed.

Pass on secondhand compliments to your spouse.

Make lists of what you both need to do
and then prioritize those activities to make plenty
of time for each other.

The sense that someone else cares
always helps because it is
the sense of love.

George E. Woodberry

Consider going on a Club Med vacation
to spice things up a bit.

∽

Believe deep within your heart
that you deserve to be happy.

∽

Don't put your personal happiness on
the back burner because of your mate
or your children.

HOW TO ROMANTICALLY
VACATION TOGETHER IN SPITE OF
HAVING CHILDREN ALONG

• ———————— •

Reserve separate but connecting rooms for
  you and your children.
Bring along a baby-sitter to allow you some
  privacy.
Go on a cruise that is specially designed for
  parents and children.
Rent a condo or vacation home that will
  allow for more time alone with your
  mate.
Get up earlier than your kids.
Stay up later than your children.
Consider leaving the kids at home with
  grandparents on your next vacation.

To keep a lamp burning,
we have to keep putting oil in it.

Mother Teresa

Split up all yucky household chores.

∽

Go camping in your own backyard for something
different and to get out of your daily grind.

∽

Remember that two heads can be better than one
when making big decisions, so appreciate
having someone to talk things over with.

∽

Play make-believe games with your mate.

Always try to put a positive spin on the things
that drive you crazy about your mate.

Happiness is a by-product of an effort
to make someone else happy.

Gretta Brooker Palmer

Imagine your lives together at twenty-five,
thirty-five, forty-five, fifty-five, sixty-five,
seventy-five, eighty-five, and ninety-five.

Imagine your life without your mate at twenty-five,
thirty-five, forty-five, fifty-five, sixty-five,
seventy-five, eighty-five, and ninety-five.

Write out a short essay on why you are special
as a little reminder of your own value.

Say kind things to yourself every time you look
in a mirror to boost your self-confidence.

Tape record your feelings of love and tuck them
in your mate's suitcase when he leaves
on his next business trip. Just be sure that he
has access to a recorder.

There is no value in life except what
you choose to place upon it, and
no happiness in any place except
what you bring to it yourself.

Henry David Thoreau

What do your parents think about your mate?

What do your in-laws think about you?

How does this all impact your relationships
with your own family, with your in-laws,
and with each other?

What do your children think of your marriage?

What do all these observations tell you about
your marriage?

Place your best wedding photo in a place of
honor for all to see.

Have your mate's picture on your desk at work.

To be upset over what you don't have
is to waste what you do have.

Ken Keyes Jr.

REASONS TO PLAY TOGETHER

• ———————— •

It keeps you young.

It helps you maintain your sense of humor.

It fills your life with joy.

It relieves stress.

It makes you feel free.

It helps you to get in touch with your inner
child.

Wear your wedding band at all times.

Write compliments on Post-It notes and place them
all over your home for your mate to find.

Take vacations that allow you both to indulge
in your hobbies or interests.

Several months before you take a vacation,
rent travel videos, and get travel magazines
and books to build up some excitement
about your upcoming trip.

What things would your children change
about your marriage?

Reflect on these. Are they realistic changes
you can make for the sake of your family?

Consider being celibate for a bit before going
on a second honeymoon.

PHRASES TO USE WHEN TALKING
TO YOUR MATE

•————————•

"Thank you."

"That's better."

"Congratulations."

"I'm proud of you."

"I appreciate your help/efforts."

"I couldn't do it without you."

"That's a good point."

"We are going to make it."

Sit side by side in rocking chairs
and get reacquainted.

Talk happiness. The world
is sad enough without your woe.
No path is wholly rough.

Ella Wheeler Wilcox

Relax and play with your dog together.

❧

Write poems that express your feelings about:
marriage
love
sex
your mate

❧

Save the good fortunes from
Chinese fortune cookies and wish these
for your mate, yourself, and your relationship.

Pray for wisdom.

HIRE SOME HELP SO YOU CAN HAVE MORE TIME WITH YOUR MATE

Hire a housekeeper or a cleaning service.
Get a lawn service to do your yard work.
Find a good baby-sitter for the kids.
Get a cook to prepare your meals.
Hire a service to clean up after your pets.

Stop being a couch potato.

Remember that your opinions
are not necessarily factual.

Catch your mate doing something good and
show your appreciation.

Stop saying *always* and *never*.
Those words just lead to trouble.

Be rational even in the midst of a crisis.

Keep in mind that we all have personal problems
and try to be sympathetic to your mate's burdens.

Remember that some hurts take time to heal. Don't
rush the healing process.

Be nice to your mate's coworkers.

Show respect for your mate's boss.

∾

Take full responsibility for your:
happiness
share of the marriage

I am happy and content
because I think I am.

Alain-René Le Sage

Remember that you, your mate, plus God can
handle any troubles that come your way.

∾

Give your best to your marriage every day.

Put more into your relationship than you take out.

∽

Help each other and then help each other
even more.

∽

Try to make "working" on your marriage fun.

Gratitude is the memory of the heart.

Massieu

Smile whenever you first see one another.

∽

Always keep your word to your in-laws.

MOVE YOUR MARRIAGE UP A NOTCH THROUGH

• ———————— •

better sex
better communication skills
more time alone together
more laughs
Just pick an area and get to work!

The bravest are the tenderest.
The loving are the daring.

Henry Wadsworth Longfellow

Ask your best friend to inspire you and
keep you on the right path when you are
feeling down about your marriage.

Teach yourself to have romantic:
thoughts
actions
words
attitude
. . . to keep the home fires burning.

WATCH OUT FOR THESE ROMANCE BUSTERS

lack of caring
poor health
PMS
chemical imbalances
lack of energy

Have a fireplace in your den or living room to
inspire great late-night chats.

Perfect kindness acts
without thinking of kindness.

Lao-tse

Replace the words *can't* and *try* with *can* and *will*.

∽

If you are getting too many telephone calls
in the evenings, get an unlisted number.

∽

Get a credit card that gives airline miles and use
them for a great romantic getaway.

∽

Show your mate total acceptance.

Write out the bottom-line needs that you expect
from your mate.

How reasonable are those needs?

The future belongs to those who
believe in the beauty of their dreams.

Eleanor Roosevelt

Seek to understand your own shortcomings
and bad habits.

Take pleasure in your mate's accomplishments.

Keep in mind that true love looks past:
hard times
conflicts
hurts
disappointments

Ask your mate to write out her bottom-line needs
that she expects from you.

How reasonable are these needs?
Can you meet them?

Love should be your way of life if you want
to have a great relationship.

Only emotionally healthy people can make
an emotionally healthy marriage.

Healthy marriages require all
of the following:
respect
love
honesty
responsibility
commitment
time
How many of these does your relationship have?

෧౿

Ask yourself if you like, love,
or just need your mate.

෧౿

Great marriages are not built solely on excitement.

෧౿

Feelings come and go, but your vows
must remain intact.

WHAT TO DO WHEN YOUR MATE GETS ON YOUR NERVES

• ———————— •

Spend some time apart.

Change your activities.

Look at your mate from a detached point of view.

Invite some company over.

Distract yourself.

Ask her to stop doing the behavior that is annoying you.

Remember your own shortcomings. Your mate's might not be so bad compared to your own.

Plan a really great date that you both will enjoy and do it immediately.

Use humor to melt tensions.

When the newness of the relationship begins
to fade, you must dig down deeper to learn more
about each other.

MODERN ANNIVERSARY GIFT SUGGESTIONS

First—clock
Fifth—silverware
Tenth—diamond jewelry
Fifteenth—watches
Twentieth—platinum
Twenty fifth—silver
Fiftieth—gold

Do what you know you should do and what you
know to be right for your relationship even when
you don't want to do it.

The great secret of a successful marriage
is to treat all disasters as incidents and
none of the incidents as disasters.

Harold Nicolson

Get on the Internet and look for:
fun activities in your city that would make
for a great date with your mate
articles of interest on improving your relationship
great travel deals for a fun getaway
unusual gifts for your spouse

Talk about what you are learning about each other
from this book with your mate.

Always pick up prescription medication for your mate when she is sick and bring along a little get-well gift.

∽

Even when you know that your mate is wrong, refrain from calling your spouse a liar.

∽

Don't use sarcasm.

∽

Validate your partner's feelings and point of view, even when you disagree with them.

The best argument is that which seems merely an explanation.

Dale Carnegie

UNDERSTAND THE FACTORS THAT WORK AGAINST MARRIAGES IN OUR SOCIETY

• ——————— •

We have a very quick-fix mentality.
Divorce is accepted as a normal part of life.
Spouses are overwhelmed by careers and
    kids.
We place enormous value on youth, beauty,
    and wealth.
Marriage and fidelity are often viewed as
    out of date.

When you hug, embrace each other fully
to really feel connected.

Give your spouse enough emotional
and physical space.

When you hit the empty nest period:
Rebuild your relationship.
Rediscover your partner.
Get remarried to each other and invite the kids
to stand up for the two of you.

TIPS FOR STEPPARENTING

• ———————————— •

Take things slowly with the children.
Don't try to force a relationship. Let things
    evolve in their own time.
Be kind, but firm.
Let the children decide on what to call you.
Remember that this is an adjustment for
    everyone, not just you.
Spend time alone with each of the children.
Plan activities that the whole family can enjoy.
Try not to get sucked into arguments.

Refrain from making any negative
comments regarding either of their
biological parents.

Remember that most stepfamilies hit problems in their relationships and many of
the troubles fade away. It just takes time,
patience, and love.

Reassure the children that you aren't trying
to replace their other parent.

Try not to disrupt their routines.

Do not involve them in your arguments with
your mate.

Seek professional help if the problems are
serious or persistent.

Hang in there when your partner seems distant.

Keep extra busy when your mate is distant.

Play games together.

Take a class together to learn something new.

Remember, your partner won't know
what you need unless you tell him.

Look for your mate's inner beauty.

Appreciate your mate's outer beauty.

Never hurry through sex unless you both want to.

Share at least one long, passionate kiss every day.

Life is not simply holding a good hand,
Life is playing a poor hand well.

Danish proverb

Eat lots of meals together during the week
to stay in touch.

The best things in life are never rationed.
Friendship, love, and loyalty do not
require coupons.

G. T. Hewitt

Begin doing more enjoyable activities together.

Travel to romantic destinations instead of
going to family-friendly locations when the
two of you take a trip.

∽

Put your marriage before your career.

The Promised Land always lies on the
other side of the wilderness.

Havelock Ellis

Learn to go with the flow, unless the tide gets
too rough—and then start making some
positive changes.

∽

Take pride in your appearance.

When you are fighting, ask yourself if
you are secure enough in your position
to listen openly to your spouse.

∽

Look at your marriage through other peoples' eyes.
Pretend you are:
a stranger watching you on a date
your best friend
your boss
your minister
your children
a marriage counselor
your parents
your neighbors
How does your marriage look from the outside?

∽

Make sure that you both always have something
enjoyable to look forward to.

WAYS TO MAKE HOLIDAYS MORE ROMANTIC, JOYFUL, AND EASIER

Keep things simple.

Let everyone take part in the planning and activities in your family.

Remember that you aren't Martha Stewart and even Martha has lots of help.

Schedule important events and let go of the rest.

Talk over "couple" plans with your mate out of earshot from the kids.

Ponder what you want each holiday celebration to be like.

Remember that you are making memories for better or worse.

Don't overspend.

Use candles for decorations. They always add a touch of romance.

Try to add beauty to your surroundings
    even if it is just a single red rose on
    your dinner table.
Plan time to unwind just for yourself.
Take lots of photos to capture the magical
    moments.
Let go of your unrealistic expectations.

Never throw away your mate's stuff without
checking with your mate.

The deepest principle of human nature is
the desire to be appreciated.

William James

Don't snoop through your lover's things.

The heart is wiser than the intellect.

Author unknown

Go out to different restaurants instead of
the old standbys.

Go out with different people instead of
your same old crowd.

Treat your mate better than you treat
your best friend.

Appreciate all of the good things that the two of you have going, both individually and together, before it is too late.

ACT LIKE KIDS TOGETHER—TRY:

flying a kite
eating a meal of just desserts
playing in the snow
going to a playground
baking cookies
strolling through a toy store

Have a friend plan an exciting night out for the two of you from time to time.

House-swap with other couples for a free vacation.

Go out on different night of the week.
Don't just wait for Saturday.

Spend the night at a lovely hotel in your own home-
town for a change of pace.

Sleep together in a different bedroom at home for a
little change of routine.

Ask yourself how your hero would solve
your marital issues.

List the habits that you need to change to
improve your self-esteem.

Pick one and work your way through the list.

Those who love deeply never grow old.

Author unknown

THE BASICS OF GIFT GIVING

• ———————— •

Make it personal.

Make it memorable.

Wrap it beautifully.

Buy what you think your mate wants.

Be extravagant when you can.

Keep track of gifts that you have given in
the past so that you don't give the same
thing again.

Look for gifts throughout the year so that
you can produce that special one when
the occasion arises.

Put lots of thought into the gift.

Forgiveness is the final form of love.

Reinhold Niebuhr

Create a fun jar that holds little strips of paper
that have things like kisses, hugs, chat sessions,
and walks written on them. Let your mate
draw out one whenever the mood strikes
and honor the inscription.

Keep a record of the positive changes you have
made in your relationship and the difference
they have made.

Stop the sad notion of trying to get even
when your mate lets you down.

As a couple, contribute to those in need.
Your self-esteems will increase, your outlooks
will improve, and your worlds will expand.

And now here is my secret,
a very simple secret: It is only with
the heart that one can see rightly;
what is essential is invisible to the eye.

Antoine de Saint-Exupéry

When you are going through an extremely busy
period, schedule at least short periods of time
to get together so you don't totally lose touch.

Ask yourself if you are behaving in a way
that represents the person that you want to be.

Think long and hard about the effects of your
behavior on your mate and children.

Make sure that you fully understand what
your mate is wanting to share with you
by asking questions to confirm the basic idea
of what he is telling you.

Remember that by working on your
marriage today, you and your mate are building
a brighter future for yourselves.

When you make any big decisions, try to wait a
reasonable period of time before taking action.

Refrain from taking every rejection personally.

Write out your hurts, problems, and any
lingering resentments.

Now write out steps to rid yourself
of those problems.

Now pick one and start working on it.

Understand that things will change over time
for either better or worse.

Make a date jar. Write down ten activities each
and place them in a little jar. The next time
you can't decide what to do for an evening out,
just draw a suggestion from the jar.

Wear gorgeous nightclothes.

Don't talk for twenty-four hours.
Either write out your feelings or act them out.

Say "I love you" ten times in the next week
and just see what happens.

Try a fabulous new fragrance.

One who walks the road with love
will never walk the road alone.

C. J. Davis

Say two or three nice things to your mate
every single day.

GOOD TOPICS FOR
DINNER CONVERSATIONS

•————————•

areas of common interests
funny stories that you've heard recently
good news
interesting current events
plans for upcoming dates together

Feed each other from time to time.

Hold hands during really tough arguments
to keep things from getting out of hand.

Do role reversal on the household chores
for a month.

Pretend to be each other and then try to have
a serious discussion. It will relieve some of
the tensions and you might learn a little bit
about how you come across to your mate.

Dress in a totally different style when you go out on
a date with your mate for a bit of a change.

Pretend to be total strangers on your next evening
out and learn about each other all over again.

Take unfair criticism with a grain of salt.

Refrain from dwelling on the negative events
of your past.

WHAT *NOT* TO DO WHEN YOU ARE TRYING TO IMPROVE YOUR MARRIAGE

•———————•

Listen to naysayers.

Give up.

Slack off in your efforts because you
   haven't seen any results just yet.

Become discouraged by setbacks.

Go against your intuition.

Seek help from people who are unhappily
   married themselves.

Forget to pray.

In judging others, folks will
work overtime for no pay.

Charles Edwin Carruthers

Marriage resembles a pair of shears,
so joined that they cannot be separated,
often moving in opposite directions,
yet always punishing anyone who
comes between them.

Sydney Smith

Enter contests together. It gives you something
to talk about and dream about.
And you just might win.

Argue in the nude. Your anger won't be as severe
or last as long.

Argue in a closet. That way you will
solve things very quickly!

Bring a sense of play to your sex life.

THINGS THAT WIVES CRAVE

• ——————————— •

more help with the kids
more help around the house
more time spent together shopping
more time spent talking about your
    relationship
more time snuggling

THINGS THAT HUSBANDS CRAVE

• ——————————— •

more quiet time after work
sleeping in later on Saturdays
more time spent on favorite activities
more variety in sex life
more appreciation from spouse

We pardon to the extent that we love.

La Rochefoucauld

Be five minutes early for dates with your mate.

∽

Learn to bite your tongue when
you know what you want to say will hurt
your mate's feelings. It doesn't need to be said.

∽

Think "win-win" while having a disagreement
to get the right focus.

∽

Show compassion for your mate's
childhood hardships.

Be a low-maintenance spouse.

Without a family, man, alone in
the world, trembles with the cold.

André Maurois

Make a list of the things your mate could do
to make you fall in love all over again
and give it to him soon.

Share details about areas of your life that don't
include your spouse, like:
work
time with friends
hobbies
time alone with your family

WHEN TO SEEK PROFESSIONAL HELP

• ———————— •

You or your mate have confessed to an affair.

You or your mate are considering leaving
the marriage.

Physical abuse has taken place.

Emotional abuse has become part of your
relationship.

You are drifting apart and can't get back
together on your own.

You or your mate are unhappy.

Your needs aren't being met.

One or both of you have an alcohol or drug
problem.

One of you is going through a serious
personal crisis.

Your children are disrupting your home life.

Test your perceptions regarding your mate's:
feelings
plans
ideas

The risks of love are higher than
most investments. The rewards are
greater than winning a sweepstakes.

Author unknown

Watch for trouble signs. It is easier to put out
an ember than a blaze.

Spend at least twenty minutes a day
really being together.

Refrain from taking calls during:
meals
intimate moments
important talks
arguments

∿

Try to keep up with your home maintenance
so that it doesn't overwhelm you both.

∿

Stop looking at your mate to be Mr./Miss Perfect.
Accept that he or she is Mr./Miss Right.

∿

Don't have a roving eye.

∿

Choose the type of marriage you want.
Don't copy someone else's.

Don't just let it evolve on its own, but make a conscious decision about your style of marriage.

Take away love and our earth is a tomb.

Robert Browning

MARRIAGE CHECK-UP

Do you ever consider divorce? Are you both
  happy?
Does coming home after a hard day feel
  good?
Do you look forward to seeing your mate?
Do you love your mate?
Is this what you wanted in your marriage?
Is your mate happy?
Do you enjoy being married?

Anger ventilated often hurries toward
forgiveness; anger concealed often
hardens into revenge.

Edward Robert Bulwer-Lytton

THE TEN GOLDEN KEYS OF MARRIAGE

•————————•

love

respect

appreciation

honesty

communication

validation

spiritual foundation

shared interests

trust

good sex

Allow your mate to save face.

❧

Think twice before going to work for your in-laws.

We must strengthen, defend, preserve,
and comfort each other.

John Winthrop

Make Sundays a day of worship and relaxation.

❧

For one week notice something
new each day about:
your relationship
your love
your feelings

Cultivate a thankful heart.

Set a high value of spontaneous kindness.

Samuel Johnson

Be honest with yourself.

Release the wonderful you that is buried
under your responsibilities.

Remember that it doesn't matter where
the two of you have been. It just matters where
the two of you want to go.

Act like happily married people act.

Take charge of your:
relationship
life
self
family life
spiritual life

Failure is merely another opportunity to
more intelligently begin again.

Henry Ford

Subscribe to romantic newsletters
to get fresh ideas for your marriage.

What are your biggest fears about
your relationship?

Share these with your mate. How can the two of
you avoid these?

It is not enough if you are busy.
The question is,
"What are you busy about?"

Henry David Thoreau

Burn your bridges with anyone that you
feel strongly attracted to romantically,
other than your mate.

Take a marriage sabbatical to recharge.

239

Always look at the big picture.

Be agreeable. It will make a world of difference.

REASONS TO WORK ON YOUR MARRIAGE IF YOU HAVE CHILDREN

•——————•

Children model what they see. In other
   words, your child's marriage will
   resemble yours.
Happy marriages make kids feel secure.
Happy relationships help to produce happy
   kids.
Children learn about love, sex, and romance
   from their parents.

Keep your careers from invading your bedroom.

Create a positive self-fulfilling prophecy for your
time with your mate this weekend and see how
much better things can go.

THE MAIN REASON MARRIAGES DON'T IMPROVE

•━━━━━━•

Couples become satisfied with the status
quo.
Change frightens people.
People talk about change, but they never
start the process.
They don't want to make the effort.
Some changes take time and they give up
too soon.
People don't place a high enough value on
their relationship to do the work.

An ounce of action
is worth a ton of theory.

Friedrich Engels

∽

Refrain from empty:
apologies
promises
compliments

∽

Pray to be a good spouse.

∽

Say please.

∽

Pray together for your friends' marriages.

If you are on a tight budget you can still
be romantic:
Go on a moonlit picnic.
Stargaze.
Dance at home by candlelight.
Read poetry to each other.
Snuggle on the couch.
Rent the latest love story video.

If things are ever to move upward,
someone must be ready to take the
first step, and assume the risk of it.

William James

Find the calm spot in the center of the storm
when trouble hits so that you won't be
thrown off course.

Be a good example of a happily married couple
for your friends. It might just be what they need to
keep things on track in their relationship.

Being kind is the first order of loving.

C. Rickert Lewis

Never take the role of being a victim
in your relationship.

Love is a little blind; when we love
someone dearly we unconsciously
overlook many faults.

Beatrice Saunders

QUESTIONS FOR MARRIED PARENTS

• ———————— •

Are your children seeing love and respect
   in your relationship?
Are they seeing you both being affectionate
   with one another?
Are they seeing appropriate romantic
   gestures?
Do they view your marriage as a joy or
   duty?
Are they seeing equality of the sexes?
Do they make negative or positive
   comments about your marriage?
Do they hear you say good or bad things
   about your mate?
Would you want your children to have a
   marriage similar to yours?

Change clothes and get comfy when you come
home from work.

A kind word is like a spring day.

Russian proverb

Write about what you have learned
through the years about romantic love.

Share this list with your spouse.

Nothing happens unless first a dream.

Carl Sandburg

Allow your mate to talk for herself.
Don't put words in her mouth.

MARRY:

•———————————•

unite
join
couple
bind together
Just a little reminder what it is all about!

HOW TO OFFER CRITICISM,
ONLY IF YOU MUST

•———————————•

State a positive or two before beginning.
State your criticism kindly.
State another positive.
Request the change you are seeking.
Hug and reassure your mate.

The greatest part of our happiness or
misery depends on our dispositions
and not on our circumstances.

Martha Washington

Accept that some of your marital issues may
be due to your own poor behavior.

Speak when you are angry and you'll make
the best speech you'll ever regret.

Lawrence J. Peter

Stop trying to punish your mate.

Make a list of the chores you would have to do
if your mate wasn't around.

Does that make you appreciate your spouse more?

Imagine how hard your life would be without your
spouse if you are a parent.

Imagine the loneliness you would experience
if you didn't have your partner.

Let God love you through others and
let God love others through you.

D. M. Street

Get your ego out of the way of your relationship.

Don't hide your troubles from your mate for it will
bring a distance to your relationship.

Do more of what works.

Grow old along with me!
The best is yet to be,
The last of life, for
which the first was made.

Robert Browning

Stop making judgments about your mate
based on the behavior of her relatives.

Soul search when you need:
answers
direction

∽

Give your wife your jacket on a cold night.
Little things mean a lot.

∽

Buy a tandem bicycle and ride around
your neighborhood.

∽

Write out all love letters by hand, not by computer.

Forget injuries;
never forget kindnesses.

Confucius

Take notice of what your mate is:
wearing
doing
saying

Love is repaid by love alone.

Saint Thérèse de Lisieux

Keep in mind that if you were exactly alike,
you wouldn't need each other.

Stop seeking your mate's approval all of the time.

Draw a life map together.

Move closer to your families
to enhance your support network.

BEWARE OF THESE SURPRISING STRESS POINTS

• ———————————— •

vacations
holidays
pregnancy
finishing school
one spouse goes back to work
promotions
reconciliation with mate

Love in the past is only a memory.
Love in the future is a fantasy.
Only here and now can we truly love.

Buddha

Never give away your personal power.

❧

Add a touch of whimsy to your days and nights.

❧

Every single day, decide what will help your
romantic life the most and do it!

WHEN TO START IMPROVING
YOUR LOVE LIFE

• ——————— •

You feel restless.

You feel bored.

You are overly tired when you are with your
mate.

You feel unsettled, but don't know why.

Your body feels tense.

You can't seem to communicate without friction.

It is only possible to live
happily-ever-after on a day-to-day basis.

Margaret Bonanno

Practice being grateful for what you have *now*.

Stop blaming all of your troubles
on your poor mate.

Write out five ways to simplify your lives.

Now start working on these.

It is never to late to try in your marriage!

Little things affect little minds.

Benjamin Disraeli

Cut down the number of hours
you spend at the office.

Ask your children to help out more
around the house.

Explaining love is like explaining poetry.

Michael Drury

Cherish the good times.

Learn the difference between dependency
and healthy, real love.

THE TEN QUALITIES SPOUSES
ADMIRE MOST IN THEIR MATES

sense of humor
positive outlook
sense of fun
intelligence
compassion
honesty
loyalty
generosity
empathy
great religious faith

Refrain from gender bashing.

Role-play to learn:
your mate's point of view
different ways to solve problems

~ᔑ

Remember that when big changes occur,
they are always followed up by little ones.
Prepare yourself.

Families remember to love one another
as cherished traditions unfold.

Jan Miller Girando

Keep theatrics out of your relationship. If you
want romantic drama, read a romantic novel.

~ᔑ

Write out your wishes for your home life.

Try to rid your life of the:
clutter
rushing
disruptions

~

Give your mate a copy of *your* favorite:
book
movie
CD
poem
That way he will know what makes you tick.

~

At the beginning of each year,
mark your calendar with:
anniversaries
birthdays
special occasions

At the beginning of each month,
mark your calendar with:
dates with your mate
family functions
romantic getaways

Your heart often knows things
before your head does.

Polly Adler

Work together to be great parents to your children.

When one stops wondering at the
wonderful it stops being wonderful.

Chinese proverb

Help your mate to have a festive holiday mood
for all special days.

⌒◞◟⌒

Go on dates together that allow for lots of
time to talk, like:
strolling through art galleries
visiting museums
stopping for a drink at a coffeehouse
attending a local arts festival
picnics
leisurely meals

⌒◞◟⌒

Keep a trip diary of all of your romantic getaways
and vacations and read through it together
from time to time.

⌒◞◟⌒

Remember that life is short!

A house is not a home unless
it contains food and fire for the mind
as well as the body.

Margaret Fuller

Spend lots of time chatting on your:
deck
front porch
screened-in porch

∽

Chat with your mate instead of napping
on long car trips.

∽

Keep your romantic traditions going
and always be adding new ones.

Keep in mind that *these* are the good old days.

Agree to disagree peacefully
when you can't find a solution.

Remember that it is okay to disagree.

Skill makes love unending.

Ovid

Marriage is like a journey and not a destination.

It takes two to argue.

For one week, cancel your:
civic obligations
social obligations
community obligations
And spend more time with your mate.

❧

Stop arguing over things that don't really matter.

❧

Do something offbeat and spectacular
this weekend for your mate.

❧

Keep your marriage in your prayers every day.

❧

Take it one day at a time
during the hard times.

Life has to have a sense of fun, a lilt,
a swinging of spirit.

Patricia Corbin

Count to twenty to cool down when you are angry.

❧

Do physical activities together.
It encourages men to talk to their wives.

❧

Open doors for your wife.

❧

Believe in love at ten millionth sight!

Keep in mind that your mate longs
to feel needed by you.

Be brave and cultivate a sense of travel adventure.

Two are better than one.

Ecclesiastes 4:9

Try to learn about love and romance
from people who have different perspectives
from you.

Listen to what your mate has to say
about your weaknesses, and you just might
hear some very valuable information.

Move forward, not backward,
in your relationship by setting goals.

Many of life's failures are people
who did not realize how close they were
to success when they gave up.

Thomas Edison

Find a sense of purpose in creating
a happy home life.

One of the deep secrets of life
is that all that is really worth the doing
is what we do for others.

Lewis Carroll

Ask yourself what skills or knowledge
you could acquire that would help you
to become a better mate.

∾

Don't cry over spilt milk.

UNUSUAL WAYS TO KEEP AN ARGUMENT
FROM GETTING OUT OF HAND

•————————•

Argue lying down.

Whisper.

Argue in your front yard; you won't yell for
you won't want the neighbors to hear.

Argue at a lovely restaurant during dinner.

Argue while jogging.

Never depend on your mate for your sense
of self-worth.

❧

Learn to make sacrifices for your marriage.

❧

Try to look for the feelings behind
what your mate is saying.

❧

Ways to feel more attractive:
Remind yourself of how special and
unique you are.
Dress in styles that flatter your
body type and coloring.
Smile at yourself whenever you
see yourself in the mirror.
Use positive self-talk to enhance your self-esteem.

The heart that loves is always young.

Greek proverb

Expect little troubles to happen, like:
Kids will get sick.
Work will demand more hours.
Pets will tear up stuff.
In-laws will get upset.
Plans will change.

∾

Volunteer to help your mate instead
of waiting to be drafted.

∾

Be nice to your mate's friends.

The best way to secure future happiness
is to be as happy as is rightfully
possible today.

Charles W. Eliot

Understand that sometimes even *you* will:
be wrong
make mistakes
be a complete jerk

❧

When troubles pop up, get quiet and pray.

❧

Teach your mate to treat you well.

❧

Let your conscience be your guide.

Keep in mind that you can dislike your mate's
behavior at times, but still love your spouse.

Remember that a good marriage is one of
life's greatest blessings.

It takes two to tango.

English proverb

Consider changing your career so that you
can spend more time with your mate
if you presently work lots of long hours.

Take a personal day off from work from
time to time to spend it with your spouse.

QUESTIONS TO ASK YOURSELF

•————————•

Do you have to be right all of the time?

How hard is it for you to apologize?

Do you blame your mate for your negative
  emotions or behavior?

Do you easily accept your mate's apologies?

How often do you get mad at your mate?

All our dreams can come true
if we have the courage to pursue them.

Walt Disney

Put things in the proper perspective.
Ask yourself if the troubles you have
will matter in a week, month, or year.

Believe in the possibilities of your love.

Never cover up your own light
to let your mate's shine.

Write out things that make you happy.

How can you get more of these things
going on in your life?

Nip meanspirited thoughts in the bud.

Just for one week, think only good things
about your marriage and your mate and see
what happens. Then do it for another week.

Take up a form of relaxation
that is new to you both, like:
yoga
mediation
biofeedback

We can chart our future clearly
and wisely only when we know the path
which led to the present.

Adlai E. Stevenson

Remember that just because your mate is angry,
it doesn't mean that you have to get involved
in an argument.

Develop your level of self-awareness.

Give without keeping score.
Receive without forgetting.

Schedule activities that you like to do
either with your mate or by yourself.
Increase your overall happiness level.

Take a less-is-more approach for a change.
In other words, stop trying too hard.

There is no end to the hope that is in us.

John Bowen Coburn

Make wishes together on a new moon.

MARRIAGE AFFIRMATIONS

• ———————— •

I love being married to my mate.

I meet my own needs, therefore I am a joy to
be around.

I am fully committed to making my
relationship work.

I express my love to my mate in wonderful,
loving ways.

I am easy to be around.

My mate is my lover and friend.

I bring out the best in myself and my mate.

I am positive and upbeat in all areas of my life.

I trust God to bless my marriage.

I look for the good in my mate and I find it
every single day.

I see miracles happening in our relationship.

My life is filled with love and friendship.

My marriage is a major blessing to me and
    my mate.
I live fully and completely in the present.
My love for my mate grows day by day.
I bring out the best in my mate.
Our home is filled with peace and love.
I honor my mate and our vows.
I dedicate myself to building a wonderful
    romance.
I relax and let God help us through any
    struggles that come our way.
I visualize wonderful things for me, my mate,
    and our marriage.
Our love grows stronger every day.
The best is yet to be!
Choose several affirmations and repeat them
    numerous times throughout your day,
    especially upon waking and at bedtime.

For human beings, the more powerful
need is not for sex, but for intimacy.

Rollo May

Pretend you are your mate's lover instead of
marriage partner. How would you act?

∽

Relish the differences between the sexes.

∽

Make mealtimes more enjoyable by:
varying the menu
changing centerpieces
using different dishes and china
inviting charming company
eating outdoors

Start paying attention to all of the little choices
you make each day that create the overall
tone and quality of your relationship.

Burn last year's calendar as a way to symbolize
the end of your old marriage.

Never flirt on-line.

Keep a dream journal to gain insights about
your deepest thoughts, desires, and emotions.

Have a weekly checkup with your spouse
to discuss any relationship issues.

Write out your wishes for your home life.

Write out the things you would do if you knew you
and your mate couldn't fail.

Discuss these with your mate to learn if you can
make some important changes in the near future.

We can only learn to love by loving.

Iris Murdoch

Celebrate the first day of each month.

Celebrate the last night of each month.

Love deeply without any fear.

REASONS *NOT* TO HAVE A LONG-DISTANCE MARRIAGE

• ———————— •

You have less time for intimacy to grow and flourish.

You have less time for lovemaking.

Couples in long-distance relationships often report growing apart.

You lose out on the small details of day-to-day living.

New friendships and interests develop without one's mate.

Long-distance marriages have a higher rate of divorce.

Ask yourself what activities make you feel close to your spouse and do more of them.

If we only wanted to be happy it would
be easy; but we want to be happier
than other people, which is almost
always difficult, since we think them
happier than they are.

Charles de Montesquieu

LOVE:

•————————————•

Fancy
Care about
Cherish
Desire
Prize
Favor
Hold dear to one's heart

Write out ways that you and your spouse can
strengthen your marriage.
Try one of these ideas beginning today!

If what you are doing in your marriage
isn't working, try something different.

Love is the only gold.

Alfred, Lord Tennyson

Have a "love" signal that you can gesture
to your mate across a crowded room,
so he will know you care about him.

INSIGHT-BUILDING QUESTIONS

• ——————— •

My love life would improve if we _____.

I'd be happier if I _____.

My mate would be happier if I _____.

I resent it when _____.

The very best part of our relationship is

_____.

I lose my temper when my mate_____.

I feel loved when _____.

I feel taken for granted when _____.

I'd enjoy my mate more if _____.

Our happiest time of the day is _____.
  Why? _____.

Our best day of the week is _____.
  Why? _____.

Our marriage resembles what famous
  couple's? _____.

We could improve our sex life by _____.

Our friends would describe our marriage like
_____.

The thing I love most about my mate is
_____.

Our biggest problem is _____.
I contribute to our troubles by _____.
The reason I bought this book was
_____.

The biggest threat to our relationship is
_____.

The two words that best describe our marriage
are _____.
Our relationship is headed in what direction?
_____

The taboo subjects in our relationship are
_____. Why? _____
On a scale from one to ten, I am a _____
when it comes to being happily married.

Take every opportunity to dance together.

Forgive first.

There is no more lovely, friendly, and
charming relationship, communion, or
company than a good marriage.

Martin Luther

Don't cut romantic corners.

Look for areas to compliment your mate about.

Share your pillow at bedtime and chat.

Be aware that prescription drugs
can affect your sex life.

෬◦

Always give your mate a birthday cake,
preferably one that you made.

෬◦

Welcome change. Devise plans to help make
the changes positive and easier to deal with.

෬◦

Ask your mate what she wants for:
her birthday
Christmas
your anniversary
Valentine's Day

෬◦

Remember that silence can be golden.

Celebrate the day
that you conceived each of your children.

Love comforteth like sunshine after rain.

William Shakespeare

Buy new wedding bands for your next anniversary.

When your mate is sick:
Pamper him.
Pray for him.
Try to cheer him up.
Send positive energy his way.

Give him a fabulous present for every big birthday.

Never confuse the trials of life
with having problems in your marriage.

❦

Use your mate's photo as a bookmark
while you are away on business trips.

❦

Talk up your mate and marriage to everyone,
especially your spouse.

❦

Be your spouse's biggest fan and supporter.

❦

Refrain from making jokes at your mate's expense.

❦

Send your mother-in-law flowers
on your mate's birthday.

Apologize quickly when you lose your head.

Every time your mate gets dressed up
for a date with you, compliment her.

Be loving and gentle, even if your mate
isn't treating you the best. You can then
feel proud of your own behavior.

Lower your voice during arguments
instead of raising it.

Send your mate flowers on the anniversary
of the day you met.

Get to know on a first-name basis your:
florist
jeweler
candy store owner

Flowers grow out of dark moments.

Corita Kent

Leave your work behind when you go
on a getaway with your mate.

Before you consider throwing in the towel,
remember that the divorce rate only rises after
each marriage. Fifty percent of all first marriages,
sixty percent of all second marriages, and seventy
percent of all third marriages end in divorce.

Keeping Love Alive

Set up seasonal activities to do
with your mate at the beginning of:
spring
summer
fall
winter

∽

Say something kind to your mate
every single day.

You can overcome anything
if you don't bellyache.

Bernard M. Baruch

Always ask about your spouse's day at work.

Tape television programs on improving marriages
and watch them with your spouse.

෧෮

Lend an ear to your critics.
You might learn something!

෧෮

Always close your eyes when you kiss,
if your spouse is shy.

෧෮

Think twice before accepting a job that will require
lots of travel time away from your spouse.

෧෮

Stay with your spouse if she is hospitalized
to comfort her and make sure that
she gets quality care.

Remember that things do not show your love
as much as your time and attention do.

∽

Attend all of your mate's family functions.

∽

Buy little gifts for your mate's
collections and hobbies.

∽

Don't sell your mate, yourself,
or your marriage short.

Everything that irritates us about others
can lead us to an understanding
of ourselves.

Carl Jung

When your mate offers to help,
accept her help graciously.

∽

Never confuse kindness with weakness.

∽

Refrain from talking about your marriage problems
with your coworkers, especially attractive,
single ones.

∽

Rid yourself of guilt. Learn from your mistakes and
move forward.

∽

One day a week or at least once a month,
try to come home early from work
and spend some special time with your spouse.

Stop going on-line to chat with strangers!
Talk to your mate.

Let my heart be wise.

Euripides

Stop saying:
"I can't."
"That is just the way I do things."
"That is the way things have always been
between us."

We attract hearts by the qualities
we display; we retain them by the
qualities we possess.

Jean-Baptiste Antoine Suard

How Well Do You Know Your Spouse?

• ———————— •

Favorite holiday: _____

Best friend: _____

Biggest fear: _____

Proudest accomplishment: _____

Favorite teacher: _____

Dream job: _____

Salary: _____

Beliefs about God: _____

Happiest childhood memory: _____

Ideal life: _____

Favorite pastime: _____

Favorite song: _____

Boss's full name: _____

Favorite book: _____

Best gift ever received: _____

Next to you, greatest romantic love:

_____

Favorite fantasy: _____

Switch locations for serious discussions,
so you don't get stuck with one room in your home
that is always used for fighting.

Change the order in which you normally do things.
Turn dinner and a movie into movie and dinner.
Little changes can help you break out of your rut.

I like not only to be loved,
but to be told I am loved.

George Eliot

Don't talk your relationship into a romantic death.

Stop clinging.

Be sure that you send only clear signals
to your mate, no mixed ones.

❦

Treat your mate like you would
if you were still dating.

Ninety percent of all those who fail
are not actually defeated.
They simply quit.

Paul J. Meyer

Forget the "looking out for number one" stuff
and look out for your mate.

❦

Refrain from using automatic responses.

Remember that if you dwell on the good things
in your marriage, they will expand.

Politeness is a small price to pay
for the goodwill and affection of others.

Author unknown

Eat more leftovers and quick fix dinners,
so that you can spend more time enjoying
each other's company.

The supreme happiness of life is the
conviction of being loved for yourself.

Victor Hugo

Use your vacation time to benefit your marriage.

QUICK FIXES FOR THE MOST COMMON MARITAL TROUBLES

• ———————— •

Are you bored?

Go on a trip to an exciting destination.

Go somewhere in your town that you have never
    been before, but always wanted to go.

Plan an activity that gets your heart racing a
    bit, like hot-air ballooning or parasailing.

Pretend that you don't know each other and flirt.

Go out with a really fun couple.

Are you feeling unattractive?

Get a new hairstyle.

Go all out for a makeover.

Buy some new clothes.

Go on a diet.

Exercise.

Are you working too much?

Take a vacation.

Call in sick and spend the time having fun with
your spouse.

Take a three-day weekend when you can't get
away for a long break.

Look for a new position that requires less time.

Learn to work smart, not long.

Are you not having any fun with your mate?

Stop having serious discussions for at least one
week.

Plan at least one night out a week for a date
with your mate.

Lighten up.

Go out on the spur of the moment and do what
hits you.

Have sex in different locations.

Are you a couch potato?
Turn off the television.
Get outdoors.
Plan two new activities for the next week.
Entertain together.
Start an exercise program together.

Make a marriage treasure chest and include all
the special mementos of your years together.

Refrain from frittering your life away
on unimportant people and activities.

Feed your mate's ego from time to time.
If you don't, someone else just might.

WHAT COUPLES SAY THEY
WANT MOST IN THEIR PARTNERS

• ——————— •

great lover
parent for their children
life partner
financial partner
friend
supporter
spiritual helpmate

We must make the best of those ills
which cannot be avoided.

Alexander Hamilton

View your marriage as a sacred union.

MARRIED PERSON'S BILL OF RIGHTS

• ———————— •

You have the right to be yourself.

You have the right to expect your mate to be
faithful.

You have the right to expect your mate to be
kind.

You have the right to be happy.

You have the right to be safe.

You have the right to express yourself kindly.

You have the right to live your life in your
way as long as it doesn't harm others.

The tragedy is not that things are broken.
The tragedy is that they are
not mended again.

Author unknown

Be humble. Refrain from bragging about your
personal good fortune when your mate
is going through a hard time.

Allow your mate to help you instead of
trying to be a superwoman or -man.

Marvel at the miracle of love between
a husband and a wife.

Refrain from looking at television characters
as role models.

Remember that when you get sick, your perspective
may get a bit off, so cut your mate some slack.

What counts in making a happy marriage
is not so much how compatible you are,
but how you deal with incompatibility.

George Levinger

Look at your mate as someone whom
you can learn great lessons from over the
course of your lifetime together.

When things go wrong,
don't go with them.

Author unknown

Understand that your thoughts and actions build
your life in a positive or negative direction.

Write a love letter to your mate
as if you were going off to war and won't see
each other for a very long time.

✎

Find a safe outlet for your anger, like:
Hitting a punching bag
running
boxing
writing in a journal

✎

Keep discussions current—no digging up the past.

✎

Understand that your mate respects:
strength
dignity
self-worth
Stop being a doormat!

Keep in mind that the past
doesn't guarantee the future.

The doors we open and close each day
decide the lives we live.

Flora Whitmore

Write down the best five things in your marriage,
in your life, and in yourself whenever you feel
a case of self-pity coming on.

Stop enjoying getting mad at your mate.
Find healthy ways to build emotional release
into your marriage.

Stand tall. Walk proud. Show your mate and the
whole world that you matter.

After dinner tonight, write out
your joint goals for your:
children
finances
careers
personal achievements
health
parents
How can you reach these together?

You cannot do a kindness too soon for
you never know when it will be too late.

Ralph Waldo Emerson

Never, never, never,
never give up.

Sir Winston Churchill